The Noticeboard

A Quest for a Family

DENISE LARKIN

DEDICATION

To Michael and Faye.

CHAPTER ONE

"Oh my god, I can't believe you've put that photo on your wall."

"Shut up, you love it!"

"I do actually."

We cracked up laughing.

The year was 1993 and my best mate Karen Byrne and I were not long back from Tenerife. I'd had some passport pictures taken in preparation and was dead pleased with mine. I had a couple spare and Karen swiped one. She had this noticeboard in her hallway with loads of photos on it.

It was four of us that had gone to Tenerife – me, Karen, Cathy Taylor and Kim Hayward.

We were inseparable back then. Karen and I still are, having met when we were about seven. Funny how life goes though because we're not in touch with Cathy anymore and sadly, in 2019, Kim took her own life. She never did really like it here a lot of the time – she was unique, funny and sadly missed.

My standout memory from that holiday in Tenerife – was the four of us being in Lineker's Bar. (Owned and named after Gary Lineker's brother Wayne). I was wearing white denim shorts pulled really tight at the waist, as was the fashion back then, and I needed the loo. As I strutted across the dancefloor feeling like you feel on holiday in Tenerife in your white denim shorts, the DJ bellowed down the mic, "Look at her in her nappy!" The nightclub erupted in laughter. I was no shrinking violet back then, so I started heckling him, but he had the microphone and just talked over me, something about Karen's pigtails making her look like a milkmaid. Proper mugged us off. Another time, as Karen and I were walking to the beach a bloke shouted, "Oi, girls, where's Cinderella?" Karen was outraged and took a while to get over that haha, but I just thought it was really funny. Of course, the fella was no looker himself. Always the way. Good times though, of which my passport pic was a reminder, and which was why it deserved pride of place on Karen's noticeboard.

"Who's that girl next to me?"

Karen walked over to the noticeboard. "Oh, that's a girl from my old job," she said. "We shared that flat in Roman Road in Bow."

Karen had been a secretary at a modelling agency on Camden High Street. The girl in the photo had moved from somewhere up north out of the blue and came to Karen's office on the Youth Training Scheme. The YTS as it was known, was a big deal in the 80s and gave school leavers on-the-job training.

Karen tapped the photo. "They broke the bloody mould when they made her, Denise. I can't believe you two haven't met."

"Well, we have," I said. "On your noticeboard!"

CHAPTER TWO

"Can you look after this girl until we can find her another foster home?"

It was January 1967 when social services said these words to Ray and Janice Best. I was five months old, and the Bests had two natural daughters already. Jacky who was 12 and Jill who was 10. However, Ray and Janice desperately wanted a boy and having lost several babies to stillbirth or miscarriage, they finally went to Social Services to ask if they could foster one. When there weren't any boys, I was offered to them. And after having me for a little while, they got attached. Well, you do, don't you? At least you'd hope.

I was born on August 10, 1966, in Kingsbury to Maureen McKilbride. At least, I think that's her name. She changed it all the time. By the time I was born, Maureen already had two sons, Ricky and Anthony. Ricky was born first, followed by Anthony. Anthony had been given up for adoption straight away, but Maureen kept her first son with her. Anthony and Ricky had the same dad: Mr Frederick Piper. I have a different father – Dennis Dunleavy. Maybe that's where Maureen got the idea to call me Denise.

The Bests officially adopted me when I was two. Maureen actually wanted me back; she didn't want me to be adopted. But she had a lot of challenges. She was living in a bedsit where children weren't allowed and had to pretend that Ricky was living elsewhere. I can imagine that it was so, so hard on her. Unfortunately, in the end, Maureen was unable to keep Ricky who went into foster care where, I would later discover, he was abused.

I believe that my birth mother wanted a happy life. And she moved from man to man seeking security. I know how that feels, wanting a boyfriend to hug you and settle down with you. You do grasp at straws because you want that security so much.

There was never a time when I didn't know I was adopted. But it was my secret. It was never discussed, and I didn't tell a soul. I fantasized about my real mum; a glamorous woman who looked like me. My earliest memory of my adoptive Mum, Janice, is of her coming home with her suitcase after she'd left my Dad. I was six by this time. She tried to give it another go with my Dad and I vividly remember her coming down the path towards our front door.

My memories always seem to be of bad things. I really try hard to think of the good things, but I think too many bad things happened. I've delved really deep, telling myself, *surely there must be some good things in my childhood?* Like my dad buying me a rabbit. It was so cute! I had a rabbit in the garden but then when I came home from school a fox had got it. I had been so excited to come home from school to see my rabbit.

I also recall when I was probably about three and I put my hand in a bowl of hot custard that my mum was making. It blew up like a balloon. That has been mentioned to me many times over the years, with Mum saying, "Do you remember when you…"

Cuddles and Kisses? I'd like to remember those, but I didn't really have any of that from my mum even though I think she is a tactile person. But I do remember being six or seven and sitting outside in the garden with my dad looking at the stars. That was so exciting. He wouldn't really kiss or cuddle me – he wasn't the cuddly type with anyone. But we would sit there, just me and him. It started one evening when he said, "Let's look at the stars tonight." He then got a blanket and wrapped me up and we sat looking at the sky, the stars and the planes. It was amazing, so comforting. We did it a lot. He would talk and talk about the stars. Lovely, happy memories.

But those special memories are few and far between because the reality was that dad was in the pub. Every day. And I mean, every single day. That's all he did. He went to work and then the pub. I think that's what Mum couldn't deal with.

I never felt my mum loved me because my question is, *how can you leave a child you love with an alcoholic?* My memories of her are not really good. When she eventually did leave for good, I would have loved her to have taken me with her. I'd rather have been with my mum than an alcoholic father who was never there for me. Never. He had childminders for me. He had a good job. He was a builder, but all his money went in the pub. Every day after school, that's where I had to go and find him or should I say collect him!

We lived on the Watling Estate in Burnt Oak, which had originally been Goldbeaters Farm in North West London. The estate was built in 1924 as part of the post-World War One Homes Fit For Heroes campaign. This had been announced by prime minister Lloyd George just after Armistice, 1918. What George had actually said was, "Habitations fit for the heroes who have won the war." But the press, for the sake of headlines, shortened it to Homes Fit For Heroes, probably giving unrealistic expectations. People were disappointed when the reality fell short due to a lack of money, manpower and materials. It was a close-knit place as council estates often are. This having been the case when it was originally built, my memories of the Watling estate were far from that – it was friendly and neighbourly with big characters who in the main had hearts of gold and would help each other out. Dustmen, milkmen, fruit sellers, plumbers, cleaners and hard-working people I remember. Nobody was really on "the social" as it was really hard to get so as far as I remember, nobody bothered.

It was really a big London Overspill and during the late 40s and early 50s; after the second world war, families from all corners of London came to Burnt Oak to be re-housed. A new start after being bombed out, misplaced or separated. Blow ins from the East end, and South London as well as lots of Irish families. The estate was made up of wooden, metal and brick houses, where doorstops were spotless and knockers all gleaming with Brasso.

Growing up there, everyone knew everyone and although considered a poor and deprived area by some outsiders, I think it shone in its uniqueness. Everyone worked and paid their own way. I do remember that I had a lovely bedroom with a pretty lamp and a nice duvet. Posters on the wall from Athena and pink shag pile carpet. I have clear memories of the Bay City Rollers staring back at me from the walls and then replaced by the Quadrophenia film poster and The Who.

Christmas time saw the Co-Op Department store all a glitter with festive displays and books of Green Shield stamps being handed over at the tills. The many shops that lined the Watling Avenue on both sides, had windows full of bright tinsel and sparkling lights. Everyone just made an effort. As much as Burnt Oak had a bit of a reputation, everyone flocked there to shop. Where else can you boast of a Department Store, a bridal shop and its own Saturday Market!

Cybil Richards was everyone's favourite clothes store. When you handed over your cash, it would be placed into little tube that then flew through to the back of the shop along a pipe! Even back then I thought what a strange thing. Everyone bought their jeans from a shop at the bottom of the Watling, next to the launderette. The owner was a large man with a big belly and he sold just about every style there was. I remember buying dark denim drain-pipes with a white stripe down the side. Over the railway bridge at Burnt Oak Station, was a Tonibells ice cream parlour. The woman that worked in there really sticks in my mind as she was so friendly with a Purdie hair cut and always seemed to be pregnant. Next to Tonibells were some steps that led down to the stream that runs through the estate and just sitting back, was a cave. It was known as the Bat Cave and was always full of kids – getting up to no good.

I wouldn't know a soul there now as almost everyone has either died or moved out – you couldn't walk up the road back in the day, without bumping into a familiar face every few steps.

*

My sisters Jacky and Jill were older teens when Mum left and they didn't go with her. Jill was back and forth to Jersey, working as a dental nurse and Jacky was a troubled teen, staying out all night. However, as she got older, if I wasn't with a childminder, I would go to her house. Jacky married a man called Ted and I would get the bus after school to the Grahame Park estate in Hendon where they lived in a flat with their first baby, Lizzie, and later their second daughter Rosanna.

I was 10 when Ted made the first sexually abusive move towards me. There were three that I recall. Jacky was in the same room the first time, but Ted distracted her. He stood at the patio doors and told Jacky to look at the multistory carpark opposite, then he asked about his car which was parked at the top and in sight. While Jacky looked, he turned and showed his penis to me. I was terrified of him and when I slept there, on a blow-up bed in the living room, I hid under the covers.

Another incident was when Jacky and Ted had a cleaning job and myself and my friend were taken with them. Ted was in the lift with us alone and he once again got his penis out and showed it to us whilst he held it in his hand. In addition, when it was time to say goodbye, he would always do a slobbery open mouth kiss. Of course, like most children who have been sexually assaulted, I was too frightened to say anything. Plus, Ted used to beat the life out of my sister Jacky, and she was terrified, so no doubt I just kept quiet for everyone's sake. I did tell Jacky in later life though. She wasn't that shocked.

But because my dad would be at the pub every night, there were just loads of times when I had no choice but to go to Jacky and Ted's. Jill and Mike lived around the corner in a nicer part of the estate, and I went there quite a bit too, as much as I could really. It was heaven to go there. Mike was strict but lovely with it and I felt safe and content.

I went to Goldbeaters primary school – it's still there today. It's changed over the years; it's not what it was. And my secondary school was Orange Hill in Edgware. I remember a careers officer came and asked us what we wanted to do with our lives. I didn't have a clue.

CHAPTER THREE

When Mum left my dad, she moved to Tooting for a while and then Walthamstow – and from the age of 11, I went there at weekends, meeting her at Wood Green where she worked at Zales the Jewellers.

She had met Roy by the time, and I was about seven. She married him when I was 10 and I was their bridesmaid. When I used to visit, I would stay in bed for the whole weekend. Mum would bring me up my breakfast, my lunch, my dinner. She didn't mind at all. She hasn't got a bad bone in her body really. I just think that when her mum died – when I was five – it was just too much for her and the final nail in the coffin for her marriage to my dad. I would lay in bed and watch television. Sometimes we would go out to Walthamstow market to buy costume jewellery, clothes and shoes. I very much enjoyed being spoiled by her. I remember a few campervan holidays with her and Roy. I used to take Tracey Knight with me. Tracey's my oldest friend and we're still very close to this day.

In 2018, during the process of writing my memoir, I read a letter that my mum had written me in 2016. I had never felt able to open it and when I did, I learned the horrifying reality that my mum had wanted me to live with her, but that Roy who I got on well with, had said no. He felt it was too much responsibility. For many years I had believed it was her decision and I feel that she should have had the backbone to stand up for what was right and take me with her regardless of Roy and his wishes.

①

WELL NEELY
HERE GOES! NOBODY EVER REMEMBERS
THEIR PAST ENTIRELY OR IN A STRAIGHT LINE
SO I'M TRYING TO STICK TO FACTS. I DON'T
WANT TO SLAG OFF YOUR DAD BUT OBVIOUSLY
THE SITUATION BETWEEN US WAS RESPONSIBLE
FOR OUR SPLIT WHICH WAS SO DEVASTATING TO
YOU.
YOU CAME TO US IN JANUARY 1967 AS A
TEMPORARY FOSTERING BUT IT SOON BECAME
LONGER FOSTERING UNTIL MAUREEN DECIDED SHE
WOULD LET US KEEP YOU LEGALY FOR GOOD.
WE FINALLY ADOPTED YOU IN EARLY 1968.
BECAUSE MAUREEN KNEW WHERE WE LIVED
WE WERE ADVISED TO MOVE IN CASE SHE
HARRASSED US. MOVING TO BURNT OAK WAS
ALSO A BIG FACTOR IN MY BREAKING DOWN
WHILST WE WERE IN OXFORD ROAD I HAD THE
BACKING OF MY FRIENDS JOYCE & AVRIL & I
KNEW ALL THE NEIGHBOURS, ALSO MY MUM WAS
ONLY ½ AN HOUR WALK AWAY. AT THIS TIME
YOUR DAD WAS DRINKING HEAVILY & WAS
NOT HOME MOST OF THE TIME. NO JUDGING
HE HAD HIS OWN DEMONS TO COPE WITH.
I WAS SO ISOLATED AND DREADFULLY LONELY
I USED TO STOP STRANGERS IN THE STREET
& ASK THEM TO TALK TO ME. ONE DAY
AT MY MUMS I BROKE DOWN CRYING &
MY MUM SAID "YOU NEED TO GET A JOB
FULL TIME SO YOU CAN MEET PEOPLE, I
WILL LOOK AFTER DENISE FOR YOU" SO I DID
BUT AFTER 2 OR 3 WEEKS MY DAD SAID
IT WAS TOO MUCH FOR MY MUM TO LOOK
AFTER A TODDLER (YOU WERE ALMOST 3 THEN)

②

So I gave up my job at D.H. Evans.
At this time Jill was friendly with
Vivien Lavers, the family having recently
returned from Australia. Jill told Rose
Lavers of my need for a child minder
& so I spent a week at their house every
day with you so you would get to know
her. Then I got a part-time job
at Golders Green and things improved.
After about a year Zales closed the
Golders Green shop & I either had to
work at Hatton Garden with Zales or find
another job. This meant full-time.
It went well for a time then Rose decided
she wanted to go out to work herself,
so she said Val Pearson her next door
neighbour was willing to take over your
minding & by then you knew her so she
wasn't a stranger. So that was that.
Round about the time you started at
Goldbeaters School my Mum died. It
hit me like an atom bomb. That was
1971. Looking back now from this
woman. I am now I can't imagine how
I could possibly have left you with
your Dad but I wasn't right in the
head for about 2 years. All I knew was
I had to get away from your Dad.
All this time Jacky was into teen age
abandon. I also had another baby when
you were 2. Obviously didn't survive
was taken away. At about 20 weeks dead.
They sterilised me whilst they did the caesarean
section.

③

I LEFT IN 1973 - PENNILESS & DESPERATE. I WENT TO STAY WITH BRENDA A GIRL I WORKED WITH. YOU STARTED TO COME TO STAY WITH ME AT HERS EVERY OTHER WEEKEND FOR ABOUT 3 MONTHS. BY THEN I HAD MET ROY & BY SEPT 1973 WE MOVED IN TOGETHER IN THE SEMI-FURNISHED PLACE YOU CAME TO OVER TOOTING WAY, SOUTH OF THE RIVER. WE WERE ONLY THERE 3 MONTHS. THEN WE MOVED INTO MY DADS FLAT OVER THE LIBRARY IN WEST END LANE. UP TILL THEN YOU CAME ALONE TO STAY WEEKENDS BUT AFTER WE GOT TO W.E. LANE YOU OFTEN BROUGHT A FRIEND. WE WERE THERE FOR A YEAR & HAD TO MOVE OUT BECAUSE IT WAS COUNCIL & WE HAD NO RIGHT TO BE THERE. MY DAD HAD RE-MARRIED & WAS LIVING IN MILTON KEYNES AMONG OTHER PLACES WE ENDED UP IN MATLOCK ROAD EAST LONDON WHERE YOU CAME MANY TIMES USUALLY WITH A FRIEND OFTEN TRACY KNIGHT. EVERY YEAR WE TOOK YOU ON HOLIDAY TO VARIOUS PLACES. I CAN'T REMEMBER THEM ALL BUT AMONG THEM WAS BRIGHTON - BOGNOR - BIRCHINGTON - JAYWICK CLACTON & SWANAGE. WE HAD LOTS OF LOVELY TIMES WITH YOU. YOU WERE A GREAT LITTLE GIRL. LOTS OF FUN & CHEEKINESS IN THE NICEST WAY. I ALWAYS DREAMED THAT ONE DAY ROY WOULD AGREE TO HAVING YOU WITH US FULL TIME BUT HE DIDN'T WANT THE ULTIMATE RESPONSIBILITY. I NEVER IN MY LIFE EARNED ENOUGH TO BE FINACIALLY INDEPENDANT. WHEN YOU GOT TO 13 - 14 YOU NO LONGER WANTED TO VISIT QUITE

(4)

THE SAME WAY BUT WE ALWAYS SAW ONE ANOTHER. CAROL WAS ON HER OWN AT THIS TIME + WE OFTEN SPENT TIME AT HER PLACE IN ESSEX WITH YOU - SHE ALWAYS LIKED YOU + WAS ALWAYS PLEASED TO SEE YOU. ONCE YOU HAD MICHAEL OBVIOUSLY THINGS CHANGED BUT ROY + I HAD FUN BABY SITTING A FEW WEEKENDS SO YOU + MICK COULD GO OUT. ROY BECAME VERY FOND OF YOU IN THE END WE THREE FLAWED ADULTS, ROY YOUR DAD + MYSELF DID THE BEST WE COULD FOR YOU IN OUR VARIOUS WAYS BUT LEFT YOU FOREVER + STOPPED LOVING YOU NEVER. I DON'T KNOW IF THIS LOT IS ENOUGH FOR YOU BUT PLEASE IF YOU WANT TO KNOW ANYTHING I HAVEN'T COVERED PLEASE ASK ME QUESTIONS. I'M NOT PROUD OF BEING SO WEAK BUT ONE THINGS FOR SURE I'VE LOVED YOU SINCE I FIRST LAID EYES ON YOU + ALWAYS WILL I'M VERY PROUD OF THE STRONG, BRAVE + SASSY WOMAN YOU'VE BECOME - I WANT YOU TO BE PROUD OF YOURSELF TOO. YOU ARE AMAZING WHEN YOU WANT TO BE, JUST BE YOURSELF - YOU ARE UNIQUE

I read it, then texted her. "I opened the letter you sent me today, the one you sent me 2 years ago – and I am absolutely in shock. Think of the worst words and that's what I want to write. I can't believe and never knew any of this, because if I did,

17

I would never ever have been in the company of your husband, Roy. You put that you always dreamed that one day Roy would agree to having me with you both, but he didn't want the ultimate responsibility. So you would rather leave me with an alcoholic, than care for me".

"I don't understand, did you not read it at the time"? she asked.

"I couldn't at that time but that's going in my memoirs, I'm so angry," I told her. "You actually married two men, one that was an alcoholic and couldn't look after me and your second husband didn't want the responsibility of looking after me. Absolutely awful. I can't believe you were not strong enough to stand up to him and say no, she's my daughter. I never ever dreamt I would fall out with you again mum, but this feels like the last straw for me. You had better warn Carol."

Carol is Roy's daughter. I called Carol after this and said "Oh, hi Carol, its Denise, Janice's daughter." She was pleased to hear from me. Roy was older than my mum and Carol is therefore quite a bit older than me, so we weren't close. But I was compelled to speak to her as she had told me in the past that Roy adored me, and I wanted her to know the truth.

"I don't know if my mum told you that I am writing a book? But I just wanted you to know that

I have opened a letter that my mum sent me, and I found out that my mum didn't take me when she left when I was seven because Roy had said that he didn't want the responsibility of looking after me."

She didn't really react, and I just said goodbye and put the phone down. I often think that I might have had a much more stable upbringing if I had lived with mum and Roy. Maybe I would even have gone to university.

Mum didn't reply to my text. She probably thought she doesn't want to hurt me anymore, which is fine. Before the letter when I had asked her why she left me, she told me she felt that Ray, my dad, had mental health issues and wouldn't have survived without me. I'm not sure what to believe. We didn't speak for a long time after I read that letter.

But I did start taking my sertraline again that day. It is an antidepressant, but it helps with going through the menopause as well. I just think, *I'll just stay on it now.* I'm always fighting thinking, *no, I don't need it. I don't want to be one of those people on medication.* But I just think if I need it, I need it. I'd weaned myself off and then I just thought that day I texted her, *I'll just take it again.* I am not depressed at all, and I think it's a misconception that depression is the same as anxiety – I have suffered enormously with anxiety. Not depression.

Sending that text to my mum felt as if I'd relinquished some sort of burden.

CHAPTER FOUR

So, my weekends were spent with my mum Janice and my weeks with my dad Ray and sometimes my sisters. Dad was quite a soft parent, not too much discipline, mainly because he was drinking all the time. I remember throwing a party and inviting loads of people. Dad was at the pub while our house was full of teenagers smoking and drinking. By the time it was over, there were 16 fag burns in the carpet and a little mod called Penguin was sick on the couch. My dad eventually came home and didn't seem to mind. I went to another party and just left everyone there. Fancy leaving my own party and just peeing off to where the fun is.

In the early 80s there was a mod revival scene influenced by the original mod scene of the 60s. But the second time around, it was bands like the Lambrettas, The Specials and especially The Jam. The 1979 film Quadrophenia had come out – this is still my all-time favourite film. The film is set in London in 1964, when most working-class youngsters identified as mods – who wore suits and had scooters – or rockers who listened to 50s rock and roll, wore leather jackets and rode big motorbikes. The 80s Mods rivals were now skinheads instead of Rockers, this second time around. Me and Karen and our mates from the estate were known as "plastic mods" and when we were 13, we all went on the train to Great Yarmouth; without permission or train tickets. Down on the seafront, were so many mods and skinheads ready to fight it out, it got very messy with the skinheads and mods chanting at each other from opposite pubs. We loved it – the drama! We managed to stay out of the fight, but unfortunately, our friend Wayne Bryson still got beaten up. So badly that he ended up in an ambulance and I went with him. Wayne was tall for his age and was set upon by a grown man, as we were all a bit mouthy after a couple of locals had asked him what team he supported.

Despite these carefree and memorable times, the insecurity of my early years and the trauma of the sexual assaults by Ted were beginning to manifest. I was probably about 11 or 12 when I went to the doctors because I was hyperventilating. I went alone, as you could back then. This would never be acceptable now. The doctor told me, "You need to carry a brown paper bag with you wherever you go because you need to breathe the carbon dioxide back in." So, it started from there. I carried a brown paper bag with me everywhere I went, and I could not go anywhere without it. I would get them from the green grocers. All shops used them at that time. I don't think my dad knew about me and my paper bags until just a few years ago.

I was also probably about 12 or 13 when my body started developing enormous red rashes and welts. But every time I booked an appointment to see the doctor, they'd be gone by the time I got there. Dad would say, "It's because you're eating too much tomato sauce! Your body isn't used to it. You're eating too much of this and that." Clearly it was nothing to do with Ketchup and I just got on with it and got used to feeling anxious. I hardly ate anything anyway. Dad liked to cook beefburgers and chips, but I just didn't eat a lot of anything. I was very thin, absolutely tiny. But Mum and Dad maintained that these rashes were this or that random reaction and apparently nothing to do with my upbringing. No, it couldn't possibly have been the stress I was under having been given away by one parent, left by another, barely tended to by the third and sexually abused, could it? No. "It must be something you're eating," or, "You're allergic to your Panda teddy," were some of the things it was put down to.

But it was stress. No doubt. There was a vicious circle of hyperventilating, rashes and welts, and then the panic attacks really started and happened several times a month. They're absolutely terrifying. I wouldn't wish them on anybody. Anyone who has had panic attack knows. I can't believe that your body and your mind can actually do that to you. You can't explain what it feels like to someone who's never had one. It is the scariest thing ever. Whenever I have one, I find myself wishing I'd been run over by a car instead as I would rather be in physical pain than that level of emotional distress. Anything is better than mental health problems. Anything.

I remember one of my very first ones. I was in Waitrose in Totteridge with my sister Jill. My heart was beating so hard. I never knew how to control it. I was crying and she was trying to use the phone at Waitrose to call the doctor. I had them for a long time. I went to Edgware Hospital to speak to someone about it when I was 18. Once again, I went alone.

"How would you feel if I locked you in a cupboard?" the doctor asked me.

"I would absolutely go mad and break down the door and I wouldn't be able to cope with it," I told him.

"That's good," he replied. "You're normal

because that's what a normal person would do."

"Oh, okay," I said. I never saw him again. The panic attacks continued.

CHAPTER FIVE

At secondary school, my crush was Dennis Butler. You never forget their names, do you! I only went to school to see him! He used to give me a dead arm and that was good enough for me as he had touched me. But that's as far as it went. Innocent fun.

Outside of school I went to Canada Villa Youth Club in Mill Hill East. A big crowd used to go there, and it was a great place. My main friend at that time was Liza Rice but I also used to hang around with Tracey Knight, Lorraine Ramsey and Carol Johnson.

I was still in touch with Karen. We both grew up on the Watling estate but didn't ever go to the same schools. We knew each other from over the park and down the Watling Market where Karen and my other friend Sandra Kendal worked every Saturday. Karen went to Canada Villa with her mates Lizzy Wilson and Kim Hayward– who was later to became part of the foursome, along with Cathy –

the Tenerife girls! Kim, Karen and I were backing dancers in a band. There was Doug Jessop on drums and Colin Dawson – who I went out with for a bit – either singing or on guitar. Karen and I thought we were all that in our matching 60s style shift dresses we'd bought from Topshop in Brent Cross. We loved to shop, and also buying old clothes from jumble sales. We liked to look the part. I had a green leather mod coat and Karen had a burgundy one.

On the route to The Canada Villa there was a shop that we called the 9 o'clock shop. We'd look out for it from the top deck of the bus and if the lights were out, we knew it was after 9pm. No mobiles! Really, looking back I was a kid in an adult's world with no one looking out for me. I started going to The Royal Scot pub at Apex Corner. It's a KFC now. I didn't drink, I just went to be with the crowd. Everyone my age did that in those days and pubs just let us in.

But it was in a pub called The Production Village in Cricklewood where I met Mick. It was a pub with music that sold Scrumpy Cider and not much more. I remember the bits floating in it and it stank. I was with Kim McDonagh, another old friend – not Tenerife Kim – and on the way there walked under a bridge and a pigeon crapped on my head. That's supposed to be lucky. It wasn't.

Because there he was. Mick the skinhead with his shaved head, Crombie coat, trousers rolled up over his Doc Marten boots and the gift of the gab. I was enthralled by the pub, Mick, the lot. He was older, 17 to my 14, and he drove, oh my goodness…

And so, it began. Kim knew Mick and we started talking. He was funny and cocky, and we started going out. We were never apart from then on. He'd pick me up from school and take me to pubs and the youth club in Child's Hill. Near to where he lived; between Cricklewood and Golders Green. And we were happy. Really happy. Apart from the fact we were both really jealous. He was madly in love with me and extremely possessive. It was ridiculous. If I spoke to someone else, he'd go mad, and if he talked to anyone else, I went mad. We fought and argued like cat and dog.

*

Having children had never entered my head but within months of meeting Mick, my size six school skirt was really tight. I knew in the back of mind that I must be pregnant, but I couldn't face it. Eventually I went to the doctor on my own. I was in year 11, what we called the fifth year back then.

"You're at least four months pregnant," the doctor told me. I wasn't scared – and I wasn't fazed by it. I just knew I was very young to be pregnant.

I told Mick straight away. I can't really remember his reaction other than shock. I don't remember him saying either, "Get rid of it," or "Keep it." I think if he'd said get rid of the baby, it would have stuck in my head forever.

Mick's mum was great and came round to my house so that Mick and I could tell my dad together. Dad was pretty calm and said, "Well, what do you want to do?"

I said, "I can't have a baby. I'm too young."

We went to speak to someone about having a termination but as we sat there in the waiting room, Dad said to me, "You don't have to do this, Denise, I'll help you look after the baby."

I was deeply relieved, because I really wanted to keep the baby and I really loved Mick. It didn't cross my mind that he didn't really treat me that well. I wasn't mature enough to think it through. Dad and I left the clinic and that was it. I think if Dad hadn't had said that then I probably would have gone through with the termination. But I was really happy. Mick was fine, and supportive to start with although we continued to argue. Dad kept to his word and was really supportive – totally amazing from the get-go. I don't remember telling my Mum.

I left school straight away. I didn't like school anyway and was glad to get out. Dad must have phoned them. I told my closest friends; it wasn't a secret. Karen heard it from someone else, a case of, "Denise Best is pregnant." I was home schooled in a house by a lady in Edgware. There were about five other girls, but I didn't know any of them.

Mick was working in a scrap yard with his dad. It was his dad's friend's business – Butler's in Child's Hill. After I left school, I was there as much as I could be, sat in the hut drinking coffee from a polystyrene cup. The whole place was black with grease. As my pregnancy continued, so did the arguments. When I was about six months pregnant, we had a row in the Red Lion pub in Child's Hill and Mick pushed me so hard I fell over. That wasn't unusual, we had arguments all the time, screaming and shouting and hitting each other. It never stopped. We'd split up for a few days and then get back together, split up and get back together and on and on.

My sister Jacky gave me stuff for the baby as her daughter Rosanna was aged nine months then. I was very grateful for everything that she gave me.

CHAPTER SIX

Michael, as we decided to call him, was born on February 15, 1982, the day after Valentine's Day. I actually went into hospital on Valentine's Day, because I had my show. Mick had burnt his ankle on an oxy-acetylene gun that he used at work and couldn't drive, so I had to walk to Edgware General, which was a few miles from home. I remember Mick limping along beside me due to the pain he was in. Dad was at the pub.

It was a tough birth. Jacky came and at first we left Mick outside, then I asked her to bring him in when the baby was coming. Dad arrived, having had a skinful and then stayed with me the whole time too. I was in labour all day thinking how lovely it was that the baby was going to be born on Valentine's Day, but in the end, he arrived at 16 minutes past midnight on the 15th. I had pethidine and an epidural, so my memories are all quite vague.

Michael had to go into the neonatal unit for a

few weeks. He was 6lb 3oz – a good weight – but he had pneumonia and jaundice. I stayed in hospital and was able to visit him. My room was right next to the unit. After a little while, he was allowed to come into my room in a little cot to recover further. I absolutely loved him – he was so cute. I had to express my milk and remember holding the pump on my boob, looking out of the window, full of stretch marks because I was so skinny.

Mick and I never lived together. There wasn't any plan for that. I just stayed at home with my dad, and Mick stayed at home with his mum and his stepdad. Mick would come up and visit though. He was a happy, proud dad.

When I finally got to bring Michael home, I loved it. He slept in my bedroom in his cot beside my bed. There weren't any mother or toddler groups or anything like that for me to go to, but I was fine. I got into a routine. I got up in the morning and walked up to the nearest shop, which was a little Londis-type place. I'd buy loads of stuff then take it home in the bottom of the pram. People told me Tesco was cheaper, but it was right at the top of the Watling Avenue, which was quite a steep hill.

When I was out and about, I'd see my school friends coming home from school and they'd come over for a chat and to look at Michael. Everyone knew him and loved looking at him. Sometimes I would see the teachers and they'd look in the pram too. It was like having a very special dolly.

I saw Jacky all the time. She was a bus ride away, but I'd go over and stay at hers all day. She was amazing, a great support. I always thought of her as being such a strong woman. I really looked up to her. She worked as a cleaner at Hendon Magistrates Court and got me a job there too. Jill had had her son Lee by then. He was seven and I saw them as much as I could too.

When Michael was still a baby, and before I drove, I remember sitting on a bus going to Jacky's. Michael was sitting on my lap and the woman next to me asked me, "Why aren't you at school?"

"I have a baby," I told her.

She would not have it that he was mine. "No way! That's not your baby. No way. That can't be your baby. I don't believe you."

I looked so young. That would happen a lot. Even now if we're out and Michael calls "Mum" people sometimes turn round and say, "That's not your son! Why did he call you mum?"

I enjoyed being a mother. Sitting there watching Postman Pat every day. Seriously! God! I laugh now, but Michael loved it and would watch it all day long if he could. Some of my friends would ask to take him out and I'd let them take him in the pram to the shops and stuff. One girl, Lisa, whose boyfriend was a friend of Mick's, asked to take Michael to Brent Cross for the day and I let her! I can't believe I let her do that, especially because of what I'm like now – such a cautious parent. But I was so different then. I didn't worry about meningitis, choking, kidnapping. I wasn't aware of any of those potential dangers. If anything happened to Michael, I just took him up the hospital. He'd fall over and have some stitches in his leg. He was a boy and like all little boys he ran around and climbed onto things and fell off them. I was fine with it. I picked him up and gave him a cuddle. I was laidback, because I simply didn't know about things. It was so easy.

Dad was really good with Michael. He got the son he had always wanted really. Even today, they are the closest ever. My dad adores him. He was interested in Michael's life and wellbeing. He went to every single play that Michael was in at school and enjoyed that bond – this even kept him out of the pub a bit more. I visited my Mum in Walthamstow – Mick would drive me over there. She loved Michael and was very good with him. I think she looked after Michael for a night on one occasion.

Mick would stay over at ours sometimes. His mum was good too, very devoted to Michael. But she had four children of her own – Mick and then Shane, Jackie and Stuart.

When Michael was a bit older, I let him go to a playgroup. He went once, to try it for three hours, and he loved it. But then he went a second time and a little girl bit him on the bum! After that, he wouldn't go back, which was really sad. Then he started nursery at Goldbeaters school opposite our house. From there he went onto the infants and juniors, staying at the same school until he was 11.

When I turned 17, I learned to drive with an instructor who fell asleep during a lesson! My first car was a hand painted Vauxhall Viva. Mick had already taught me to drive by taking me round Wembley Stadium car park, so I only needed four lessons and I passed. He had a white Mk3 Cortina which had built in air horns and a sticker across the top of the windscreen saying Mick and Denise.

CHAPTER SEVEN

"Your own mother didn't want you. Your adoptive mother didn't want you, and no one else does either."

Me and Mick were still arguing about anything and everything and I had made the catastrophic error of confiding in him that I was adopted – the first person I ever told. Every opportunity he got he threw it in my face. The betrayal and pain was almost more than I could bear.

Eventually, when Michael was seven or eight months old, we split up. It had been on and off and on again but then it was done. We'd been together less than two years, but it felt like 10. I don't know to this day if he was faithful or not. I heard things that made me question everything. But I moved on.

When Michael was about two, Dad started babysitting for me so that I could go out, mainly at the weekends. This worked well apart from the nights where I'd say to him, "You're going to be home by 8pm?" and he'd say yes and then he wouldn't come home. I'd be all dressed up ready to go out to my usual pub – the Red Lion in Child's Hill – and then Dad just left me sitting there. It happened more times than I can remember. Sometimes one of my friends, usually Elaine Todd would drive up to the pub and bring him home, or my friend would stay with Michael, and I'd go up there. It even happened one New Year's Eve. I was ready and raring to go out, but he never came home as promised. I'm sure he genuinely wanted to help but was just in the grip of drink.

But when I did get out; Karen, Cathy and Kim and I loved the Middlesex and Herts Country club. Anyone who was around in the 90s will remember it as it was totally fabulous in its day. Karen and I went out a lot, just the two of us, and we must have gone to every nightclub in London. If it was new or cool or just an exciting place, we were there. We had favorite places like Casper's Telephone Bar near King's Cross. Talk about addictive! The seating was spaced out and there were phones on each table. The idea was to call another table anonymously, and chat to the groups of boys. The things we had to do before mobile phones and dating apps! It stands out in my memory – it would do I suppose. We would wind them up and make them do dares or actions – it doesn't sound funny now but at the time, it was hilarious.

Loads of other pubs and clubs were on the list. To name a few: Equinox, Paradise Lost, Browns, Legends, Tots, Reins, Southside (no tills just free drinks and an entry fee) Carwash, Eves, Riffles, Barnet Golf Club, The Dandylion, Ealing Broadway Boulevard, Hammersmith Palais, the Hippodrome, Bulugas. Then there was the Party Bus - it would pick us up at the Cumberland hotel in Marble Arch; where we would have drinks at the bar before climbing aboard. It was run by two lovely guys called Denis and Darren and the bus drove to several pubs and clubs through London. Crazy and amazing times. Add many more to the list and I still don't think I have even covered the fun and the laughs I had during this time of my life. We were mad and happy and crazy.

There was still a group of us who met in the Red Lion and a guy called Pete, who was a year older than me and a postman, was among them. I fell in love with him and ended up being with him for about six or seven years. He was amazing with Michael. He loved him.

Mick hated that I was with Pete who was the total opposite of him. He was so happy and positive. It was a breath of fresh air after Mick's anger. Mick was 100 per cent the wrong person for me, especially given that I was so anxious. And my anxiety would turn to fear, which could turn to anger. I was angry at the world, for sure, and even with Pete, we would still argue, but not to the extent of the ones with Mick.

Screaming and shouting was a coping mechanism for me back then. Pete wasn't like that and didn't really argue back, so we didn't get into fights like I had with Mick. Overall, Pete was a great influence on my life, and I was much happier with him. The relationship felt much more normal – at the time, anyway.

Pete and I argued mainly when other people rang him up to go out for a drink. His friends really loved him, and he was the centre of attention. People liked being around him. He was the main man in the group, funny and always smiling. Pete never used the fact that I was adopted against me, but I did have abandonment issues, which he played on, probably unknowingly. When we had an argument, sometimes Pete would take all his stuff and go to his mum and dad's house. I'd come home thinking, *where is he? He'll be home soon.* Then I'd open the wardrobe and see that his clothes would be gone. That was terrible for me. The feeling of being left would affect me very badly. I would drive to their house and beg him to come back. I was desperate, absolutely desperate. He would come back, but he did that a few times.

I don't think Dad was aware of any of the times

that Pete and I argued since he was always down the pub. But he was aware that Mick and I had a very dysfunctional relationship. He certainly would have heard the screaming and shouting so when we broke up, he wasn't that bothered. Dad doesn't really see the bad in anyone. I have to tell him that someone is a bad person.

When Mick and I broke up, Dad who had bought his council house when I was young, under the Right To Buy scheme, did a loft conversion so that I had my own living room, two bedrooms, a kitchen and bathroom, upstairs from him. I felt so secure with my own space but still having my Dad downstairs. I kept my flat very clean and had nice carpet and furniture. I was proud of it.

I tried to think about the future. Pete and I planned to get married. I even bought a wedding dress. Then Jacky read my tarot cards. She was really into them at the time and told me the cards said I wasn't going to get married.

"Of course, we're going to get married," I told her. "I've bought the dress and everything." But then Pete and I did end up splitting up. He went off to America for about a year. I started going out with my friends, having fun and enjoying myself but he came home, and we tried again. However, it didn't work out and we went our separate ways.

Through the years, Mick continued to see

Michael. Mick was a bouncer at a nightclub called Samantha's in the West End and after I broke up with Pete, I would go there with my friends, and he'd get me in for free. I wasn't seeing Karen then as she went travelling and lived in the USA, then southern Ireland for a while. At Samantha's, Mick met the DJ who was married to a woman called Debbie. Debbie came from a family who were extremely successful in business and Mick – with pound signs in his eyes – pursued her. They got together and all of a sudden Mick was living a very luxurious lifestyle, which was hard on me because he'd come round and tell me all the details about where they were going on holiday, who they were seeing and all the fabulous food they were eating.

Mick gave me £12 a week for Michael. It wasn't anything official or legal. He just came up with the figure of £12. He'd say to me, "You can buy vegetables and fruit with that," and then we'd argue at the door and end up having a fight. On one occasion, I grabbed his t-shirt, then the following week he told me, "You're only getting £8 this week because I need to buy a new t-shirt because you stretched mine." He then said that he and Debbie had discussed the situation and that I would only be getting £8 a week from then on. He was always in control of the money, and I always felt like I was begging. He had all the power and would try to cuddle and kiss me when he came to the door to drop off or collect Michael – even with Debbie sitting in the car down the road. Mick was always a chancer and to say he played with my emotions is an understatement. I just didn't have the strength to tell him where to go. If I tried, he laughed it off.

But despite mine and Mick's fights over money and various other things, Michael always had a relationship with his father. That was always important to me. I wanted Michael to see his father. I wanted him to have that secure relationship. I wanted Michael's childhood to be different to mine.

When Michael started school, I was able to work full-time and I began cleaning – three houses a day. I'd drop Michael off at school and off I would go. I enjoyed the work, even though it was cleaning. I also worked the weekends when Michael was at Mick's. I was a waitress at the RAF museum in Colindale and in Highgate at Lauderdale House. I once served Vera Lynn at the RAF museum. I took her a drink on a tray and was scared I'd spill it. Thankfully, I didn't.

Having Michael definitely saved me. A lot of my friends started taking drugs and all sorts. I know I easily could have gone down that road but having Michael kept me sane because I had something to focus on. As much as I did go out at night with my friends, I was very focused on Michael. I think that's what kept me going.

When Michael was a baby, I had one of those Silver Cross prams, a green one. Michael used to sit up in it with his reins on and he'd always be clean and spotless. I wanted people to see that I was coping well and being a good mum. One day I was walking, and I saw a girl who I knew from school across the road. She was with someone, and I could see her pointing at me, obviously talking about me. When I was younger if this sort of thing happened, I didn't really care too much because everybody knew that I had a baby, but as time went on and I got older, I started to feel deeply ashamed of being a young mum – a feeling that clearly wasn't going anywhere.

CHAPTER EIGHT

My hands shook as I clutched the paper and stared at the words. Words about my birth mother, details that I had never seen or known until that very moment.

Ricky Piper and Maureen Dunleavy.

Visit to Mrs Maureen Piper at 2 Oak Grove, NW2, on the 3rd May 1967.

Maureen is living in a small boarding house. She shares a room with a girlfriend and they have the use of the kitchen. Most of the other boarders are men and they have breakfast and an evening meal on the premises.

Maureen is five months pregnant but has threatened abortion and has been told she is unlikely to carry the baby to term. She is now 22 and this is her fourth pregnancy.

She is pale and thin and does not look particularly well. She is having intermittent haemorrhage and should not be up at all. She has told me she left Dunleavy [a person], knowing she was two months pregnant, because he 'did not want Ricky' and was preventing her from going to see him. He is extremely jealous of the boy. She knew that if she stayed with him she would never make a home for Ricky and this, she says, she is determined to do.

Maureen's mother lives in Borehamwood. Maureen is illegitimate and has never got on with her stepfather. She says her mother would have her with Ricky, but her mother's husband would never allow this. I have the impression that Maureen is genuinely devoted to Ricky in her own way. She is opposed to him being boarded out because she does not want him to become attached to anyone else. She understands the effects which her sudden bouts of visiting and then her long absences does to him and, if one had time to be constantly on the doorstep reminding her and even taking her to see the boy, he would probably get the regular contact he needs.

Maureen said she would go into a hostel with Ricky if there was a definite understanding that she would be given a flat, but not otherwise. She feels that life for a child in a hostel is even worse than having him in a nursery (he was in a nursery in Stanmore at the time). I told her that we would have to move Ricky either to a nursery or a children's home next year before he was five. Maureen said she was sure she would have him before then.

Maureen has become quite friendly with Mr and Mrs Best, the foster parents, who have even tried to find a place for Maureen and Dunleavy so that they can have the children. It appears Dunleavy would not cooperate and, in any case, would be unwilling to accept Ricky. Maureen feels that Denise has become attached to her foster parents and it would be the best thing if they adopted her. She knows they want to do so. In fact, they have asked her. Although in many ways Maureen is curiously detached about Denise, she says she could not stay away from her if she knew where she was. So the situation is that the Bests will probably have to move if they want to adopt Denise. Maureen did not waver in her decision once made to have Anthony adopted and she said she would not change her mind about Denise provided she did not know where she was. Assistant Children's Office.

The words swirled in my mind, and I tried to make sense of it all. My mother who was about the same age as me, was illegitimate, pregnant for the fourth time, sick, weak from bleeding, and on her own having broken up with a jealous man. She couldn't go home because her stepfather wouldn't have her there. She'd had Anthony adopted and was desperately trying to find a way to keep Ricky. She's described she was, "curiously detached about

Denise…" But would be "unable to stay away" from me. Unable?

I read the words that described me at the time. I am, "attached" to my foster parents and it would be "the best thing if they adopted" me. The Bests, my Mum and Dad, had tried to help Maureen.

Whoever had written this report was talking about me, tiny little me, completely powerless. Wanted but not wanted, separated from one mother, attached to another, trying to find a family and survive, knowing nothing about anything.

*

I was about 20 when I decided to go to social services to see what I could find out about Maureen Dunleavy and my brothers. As busy as I was with Michael and my friends, thoughts of my natural mother were on my mind. But where to start? All I knew was my mother's name, so I made an appointment at social services in Finchley. I wanted to know what these people looked like, what sort of lives they'd had and where Anthony and Ricky lived.

I've never felt curious about my biological Dad although recently I've been having a look online to see if anything comes up. Nothing has. Yet.

The woman at social services knew why I had made an appointment and had all the paperwork out. She went through every detail of it, read everything: you were born here, you weighed this much.

When I was adopted, Ray and Janice lived in Kilburn. Maureen would only let me be adopted if she didn't know where I went, since she didn't trust herself not to come and find me. Maureen, weirdly, had originated from Burnt Oak, which is where I then ended up living for all my upbringing – crazy to think I ended up where she was actually from.

Then the woman passed me another piece of paper dated August 29, a few months after the first document.

"Re: Ricky Piper and Denise Dunleavy.

Visit to mother, Mrs Maureen Piper, Lambert.

Now she's at 95 Melrose Avenue, NW2.

Maureen was looking much better. She has now dyed her hair auburn. She said she has not taken Ricky back to Stanmore because he had had tonsillitis at Stanmore Nursing Home. She said she was going to take him back on the Tuesday or Wednesday bank holiday. I advised her to take him to see the doctor first to see that he was alright. Ricky certainly looked very well and seemed happier with his mother than he does at nursery. He is certainly talking better. Maureen says he gives her a lot of lip. Maureen and Jack Lambert have a large room where there would be adequate space for Ricky and the baby (Jackie).

The landlord does not know that Ricky belongs to Maureen (she says) although he has seen him there. Maureen says she is going to risk it and have Ricky home when she returns from the hospital with the new baby who, at present, she intends to keep. The new baby is not Jack's; the putative father is Dennis Dunleavy but apparently Jack is going to accept the baby and Ricky, according to Maureen thinks the world of him.

Maureen says she has been to the solicitors to see about a divorce and she and Jack are going to get married. She is taking him to see her mother.

Maureen said that she would like Mrs Best to go ahead with adopting Denise, even though the date of the Bests moving to new accommodation is uncertain. If she follows the precedent she set with Anthony she will be quite sensible and cooperate about this. She and Mrs Best are on quite friendly terms and Maureen is quite a good-hearted girl who would not willingly, I think, hurt anyone. She is now anxious that adoption proceedings should start as soon as possible. I said that when the time came I would take her to Willesden County Court to give her consent. She doesn't not know where Dennis Dunleavy is living and there is no way of contacting him."

"Jackie?" I asked the clerk.

"Yes, did you know about her?"

"No," I said. "I knew I had brothers, but not a sister. That's going to be confusing," I added, trying to make light of it. "I already have sisters called Jacky and Jill."

"I'm sorry, but I don't have up to date addresses and even if I did, I couldn't give them to you." I must have looked disappointed.

"But you can take these papers," she told me. She'd Tippexed out Anthony's address, but I could see through the Tippex: 126, Watford Road, Harrow.

"Thank you," I said and I crept away. I didn't tell anybody what I'd discovered. Nobody except my immediate family and Mick knew I was adopted anyway. What could I do? I just carried on as if nothing had happened.

*

Five years after my visit to social services, I plucked up the courage to go to 126, Watford Road, Harrow. The family living there had been at the address for a while and didn't know anything about Anthony Morgan. There was a junior school opposite, and I thought that maybe he'd been a pupil there. I considered calling the school for a forwarding address, but I never did. I hired a private investigator as I knew Anthony's parents' names – John and Joyce Morgan. They sounded comforting to me. But even the PI couldn't find my brother for me. Back then, in the late 90s, it wasn't easy to find people. Not like it is now. I thought that Anthony might have gone abroad or could be in prison. It didn't occur to me that he might have died.

CHAPTER NINE

After Pete, I met a guy called Graham and went out with him for about a year. He was an insurance broker and seemed really lovely and normal. He was good with Michael. But then he moved away. But I was loving life. I had a nice car – I always had a nice car. I'd get one on HP and pay it off monthly. I was on the council housing list and got offered three different properties, but I turned them all down because I just felt so secure living above my dad. Michael liked it there and was a very happy child, funny and no trouble at all. He enjoyed school and when the time came, he transferred to a secondary school in Mill Hill. He didn't know what he wanted to do when he left school, but he did love motorbikes from a very young age. Mick bought him an off-road one when he was about 12 and they'd go out on their bikes together. I was fine since I knew he wouldn't come into contact with any traffic.

Michael and I did eventually move though – to a

flat in north Finchley, about five miles away from Burnt Oak. Dad had said he could rent out the upstairs flat for good money. I was happy to move, as long as where I was going to was nice and the Finchley flat was lovely. It was on the second floor, which was the top floor, and I felt really safe. We lived there for about five years very happily. Suddenly, different people had started to move in, some of whom were awful and played really loud music. One time a lady had pressed the tradesman's entrance button and when I went out to look, she was sitting at the bottom of the stairs. I asked her what she was doing, and she asked me if she could wash her hair in my sink!

Even though we'd moved, Michael continued to attend his school in Mill Hill. I took him and collected him each day. As he got a little bit older, he did sometimes cycle, but it was too dangerous, so I preferred to take him.

When Michael was about 11 and I felt he was old enough to understand, I picked him up from school and prepared to tell him the truth about my beginnings. I chose my words carefully. I said, "I'm adopted, and I just want you to know. I don't want it to change anything. Grandad is still your grandad."

Michael has always had a close relationship with my dad so telling him that I was adopted might have had implications for his relationship with my dad. He cried for five minutes and said he couldn't believe it. But then he said, "Mum, it doesn't change absolutely anything with me, you, grandad, nothing." It never has. Thankfully it hasn't affected him.

I didn't want him to hear it from anyone else. I'd been thinking of telling him for years and by finally doing it, I felt as if a weight had been lifted. Only now, at this age, do I know that when you talk about things, life is so much easier afterwards. I'd told barely anyone about my life. Even when I had my daughter Faye, the midwife came around to see me and Jacky and Jill were there. The midwife said to them, "You two look alike but you don't look anything like them, Denise!"

"Really?" I said and I just laughed it off because I would never say that word, "adopted". Never. I just could not say it. But now if someone said that, I'd just come out with it. It makes me laugh that people say, "You look so much like your dad!" Or "You look so much like your mum." I think, *well, that's clearly impossible.* But I would never say anything back then. Now I really don't care. But before, I hid everything, and life was one big secret for me. And all that keeping secrets did, was just to completely stress me out the whole time.

Barely anyone knew about my adoption when I told

Michael. If anybody did know, it was never spoken about. I remember one of my friends saying to me a lot later on in life, "I remember you said to me you were adopted. Are you?"

I said, "No! I was probably saying it to get attention."

I must have told her then regretted it. I hid it because I was so ashamed. It's horrible to live your life like that, worrying constantly about what other people think. Horrible.

After telling Michael that I was adopted, everything carried on as normal. I don't think he ever mentioned it again. Michael doesn't know the depths of my life, what I've been through. If he reads this memoir, he might get it more. But some people just don't understand. They think, *just get on with life, that's it.* Michael has got a very kind heart. He's very sensitive and he's very caring and I've tried not to let him see me be upset and stressed – well, stressed maybe – but not anything to do with my past life – I don't let him see anything that affects me. Not even now. I just hide it because I don't want him to worry about me. I don't want him to think anything is wrong. Maybe I'm like that because of all the stress I endured as a youngster? Maybe I just want to protect Michael, to protect people in general? I think mental health is a very complicated and sensitive subject and I keep it in my head. I wouldn't want him to know that I've had anything wrong with me because I feel that he might get it or something. So, I don't tell him anything.

I really don't know how he'll feel reading this. He might not want to read it. My dad wrote a memoir and I've never read that! I've had it in the cupboard for 12 years. Maybe one day I will. I think he had a hard time when he was younger. He came from a very big family and during the Second World War, his mum kept lots of her children with her but sent my dad away. He was evacuated. That really affected him. I don't think he was ever the same. Mum used to say he did have mental health problems, but I don't know to what extent. I don't know if that's in his memoir or not, but it might make me anxious if I read all of that.

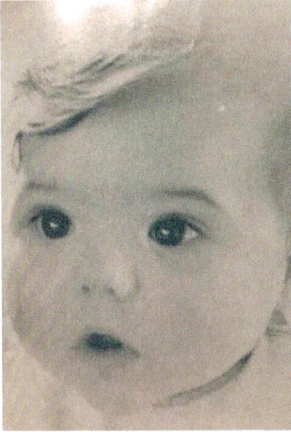

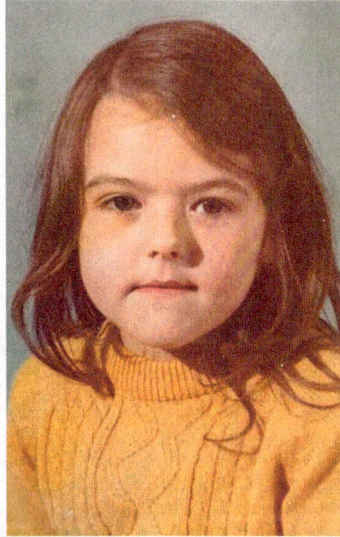

Me at five months old, above,
and right, a school photo when
I was aged six or seven

With my father, at home in Burnt Oak; and a note he wrote on the
back of my school photo to my sister Jacky, asking her to babysit me

As a baby with Jacky and her friend, and right, me at age fourteen

On holiday in Tenerife. I am on the right, with Karen (centre), Kim and Cathy (left)

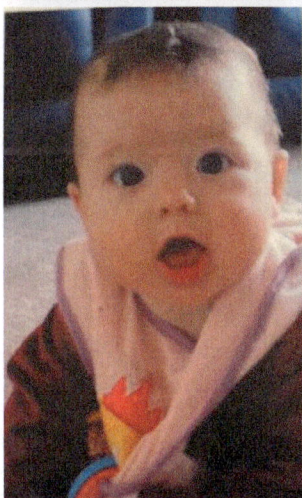

Clockwise from top left:
Michael, aged two; Michael
and Faye in Corfu, 2020;
Faye with Michael's sons,
Louis and Mikey (right); and
Faye as a baby

Maureen with Debbie and Susan, and below,
the service sheet from Ricky's funeral.
Bottom, a postcard from Ricky

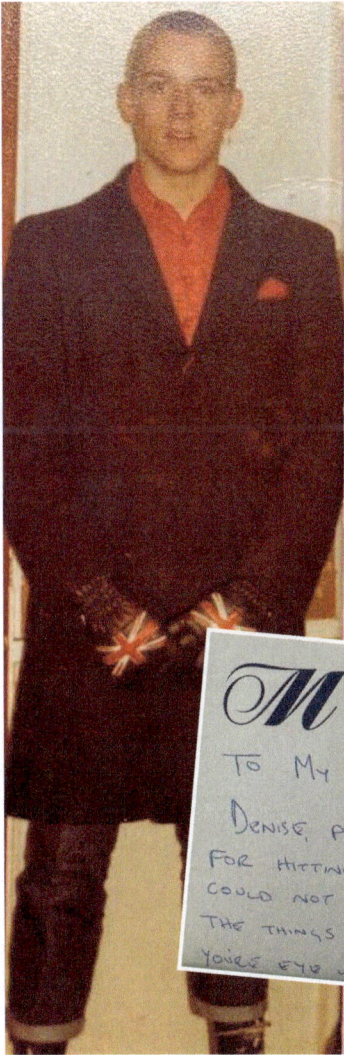

Mick when I
met him, and
below, one of
the apologies he
sent me for
hitting me

M

TO MY LITTLE ANGEL,

DENISE, PLEASE FORGIVE ME DARLING
FOR HITTING YOU LAST NIGHT BUT I
COULD NOT HOLD MYSELF AFTER ALL
THE THINGS THAT WERE SAID. I HOPE
YOU'RE EYE WILL NOT BE BRUISED OR SORE

CHAPTER TEN

"The answer is under your nose."

I looked at Jacky. "What?"

"That's what the cards are telling me, Denise. The answer is under your nose."

It was 1993 and Jacky, Jill, Karen and I were in my flat above my Dad's. Jacky was still into Tarot cards and was doing mine. She was really good at it; she had the gift you might say. I'd secretly asked her if the cards had revealed anything about my birth family.

Her telling me that the cards wanted me to know the answer was under my nose was no help at all. Karen looked at me. I knew she had no idea what me and Jacky were talking about. How could she? I took a deep breath and contained myself. "The thing is, Karen," I said. I paused, my heart racing. "I've got something to tell you."

"What?" She stared at me. She looked terrified.

I breathed out. "I'm adopted," I said. "I know it's weird that I've never told you, but it's just hard to talk about."

"Adopted?" She was stunned. "What? Oh my god, Denise. Really?"

I nodded.

"Are you joking?" she said. She shook her head. "Oh my god. I can't believe it. Hang on, does that mean you three aren't full sisters?"

Jacky and Jill nodded. Karen looked stunned. "And, oh my god, Ray isn't your dad?"

"No," I said. "Sorry, this must be a bit mind-blowing for you after all these years. Is that what the cards are on about, Jacky, saying the answer's under my nose?"

Jacky nodded. "It must be."

"Are you looking for your family then?" Karen asked.

"Sort of," I said. "I mean, I have been," I said. "Only a little bit. But I didn't get very far. My mum is called Maureen McKilbride. I went to social services a few years back to see if they had any more information. I've got brothers, called Ricky and Anthony and I wanted to find them. Then social services told me I had a sister too – Jackie."

Karen's mouth fell open. She looked totally lost. "Another Jacky?" she said.

"Yes, spelled 'ie'," I said. "Confusing or what?"

We sat in silence for a bit. Processing what had just happened. What happened next, was to change the rest of my life. A chance in a million, a moment that stands in time.

"But hang on," Karen said "You know Susan who I lived with in Bow? Her mother was called Maureen McKilbride and she had a sister called Jackie and a brother called Ricky!"

Silence. Then I managed to speak. "What?"

The room began to spin.

"Honestly, Denise. I remember her telling me that."

"What? That girl next to me in the photo on your wall?"

"Yes, her!"

"What?" said Jacky.

"Karen lived with this girl, Susan," I began.

Karen then explained. "Years back I lived with a girl called Susan. She'd come down from Lincolnshire and worked at the promotion agency with me on a YTS. She was brought up in care with her sisters Jackie and Debbie and they had an older brother Ricky. Their Mum was called Maureen McKilbride! She talked about it loads. I've never forgotten it because it was horrible for her, going into foster care. She'd lived in all these foster homes and wasn't very happy, so she came down to London."

"What's the photo got to do with it?" Jacky asked.

"Karen had a picture of her on her wall and my

picture was right next to her," I said.

I was gobsmacked. What might this mean? Jill wasn't having any of it. She shook her head and whispered to me, "Karen's just trying to get in on it."

I frowned at her, but Karen was stood up looking for her car keys. "I'm going home to see if I've got a phone number for Susan," she said. "I'll be back."

Jacky, Jill and I stood in the kitchen in a state of shock. None of us knew what to say. Did I have a sister that I never knew about that Karen had known all these years? And had she and I been next to each other on the noticeboard. Whilst I had been searching to find my birth family?

15 minutes passed then we heard Karen running up the stairs. She burst through the door with her fluffy Zebra-print Filofax. "I've got it," she called. "Fingers crossed she still lives in Kilburn."

We went into my bedroom and Karen rang the number. As it started to ring, we just stared at each other.

A man's voice said, "Hello?"

"Is Susan there please, its her friend Karen?"

He must have said she was home because Karen nodded at me. I pressed my face as close to the receiver as I could.

"Karen?" said a voice. "Blimey, blast from the

past."

"Hiya, Susan," Karen said. "Look, this is a very strange question, and I know we haven't spoken for a few years, but was your mum called Maureen McKilbride?"

"Yes," Susan replied. "Why?"

Karen looked at me and paused. "Well, my friend Denise," she continued, "her Mum is also called Maureen McKilbride. Denise has just told me that she was adopted, and as mad as this might sound, I am ringing to see if you two might be sisters. I'm with Denise now."

I stared at Karen for what seemed like hours – but was a few seconds. Then Susan said very spontaneously "Where are you? I'll get my boyfriend Geoff to bring me."

Karen gave Susan directions and I ran downstairs to my dad. "I think I may have found a biological sister," I was so excited. He stood up with a beaming smile on his face. "I'm so happy for you," he said.

"Dad, I'm on top of the world!" I said.

Meeting Susan was honestly one of the best days of my life. It was completely amazing. She walked through the door of my flat and we hugged. Until that evening, we had both had no idea that the other even existed. We just held each other and looked at each other, completely stunned I suppose.

I told her the little I knew, and Susan told me that after Maureen had Jackie, she had two more daughters, herself and then Debbie. What we did learn, was that she didn't know about either Anthony or me; and I didn't know about her or Debbie. After we'd calmed down a little bit, Susan said, "I'm going to ring Jackie." It was all happening so fast.

"Guess what, you'll never believe it," we heard her say.

Susan got off the phone. "She's in shock, but she's happy," Susan said. "I've got Ricky's number too. We're in touch sometimes. I'll call him."

Both of us had so much to take in. I couldn't believe what was happening. I had met Susan, she knew where Jackie was and now, we were going to hopefully chat with Ricky. All these names that appeared on official documents from social services weren't just a dream; it was becoming real life in front of my eyes, over the course of one evening! The only ones we couldn't contact were Anthony and also Debbie. She wasn't "on the phone," as we used to say back then, if people didn't have a landline.

Ricky lived on the north circular road at Palmer's Green. He drove with his girlfriend in his campervan, but they broke down just around the corner. He called me and I drove round to meet him. We stood and waited for the RAC. He was in total disbelief and just cuddled me. He was really happy and excited as we chatted away. I didn't ask him how he felt about our mother, but I mentioned his name as being Frederick as I had seen on birth documents – which he didn't actually know and was quite a shock to him. I also told him that my mum and dad wanted to adopt him also, but Maureen wouldn't allow it. I think he was happy to learn this, that somebody did want him.

I can't remember if Susan was with Ricky and I as we chatted, but I do remember that when Susan went home, Dad tried to give her £20 to treat herself. That's his way.

That night, Susan and I just spoke about the fact that Maureen had had six children altogether and had given them all away. Ricky, Anthony, me, Jackie, Susan and Debbie. Jackie, Susan and Debbie were all sent up to Lincolnshire – where they were fostered but never adopted. They had an awful time. It was really hard for them. So, Maureen had six children and put us all into care and as much as I can see how this happened to her, part of me also thinks: *How can you possibly get up in the morning knowing that you've done that? How can you?* Just having one child and giving it away must be horrendous, let alone six.

Jackie, Susan and Debbie had contact with our

mother Maureen when they were younger but hadn't seen her for years. She had mental illness and they all seemed quite wary of her. And none of them knew that I existed. I was older than all of them. Gone. Adopted. Never spoken of. But none of that seemed to matter anymore. What was it Jacky had said the cards were telling me? That the answers were under my nose. They truly were.

CHAPTER ELEVEN

Karen and I went on to spend a lot of time with Susan and we were at her house a lot over the next few years. We also went on holiday during this time, together with Kim Hayward, Sandra Kendall and another friend called Hayley. We went to Karen's Dad's caravan at a Haven site in Winchelsea. We had a massive sand and mud fight that day on the beach and were all covered in black muck. It was a lovely period of our lives.

Karen was really good friends with Susan and actually had a closer relationship with her than I did. It wasn't like we were sisters somehow, even though we were. It was more like we were friends, but then we hadn't grown up together.

I drove to Boston in Lincolnshire with Jill to meet Jackie and Debbie which was a surreal moment. To be seeing Jackie for the first time – a baby that was referred to in my adoption papers – part of my actual past, was incredible. And the finding of them having been such a one in a million coincidence in the first place, was so amazing to think about. Meeting Susan was also a great moment, but I didn't have time to process it. One minute I was telling my story and the next she was on my doorstep. But with Jackie and Debbie, I had time to think it through. It was a mixture of nerves and happiness rolled into one.

We all met in Horncastle near Boston. Debbie seemed quite a happy sort of person, very jovial – a bit like me, and she just took it all in her stride. She was just joking about, as if we'd known each other for ever. She had a young son. Jackie also seemed happy to meet me. We chatted about lots of things.

Not long after my first visit to Boston, Karen and I went back up there for a weekend. We drove to Jackie's house to meet with Susan and Debbie. That night we all went out to a nightclub and then back to Jackie's house to stay over. Jackie, Susan and Debbie started arguing and didn't stop. Apparently, they had always argued. Perhaps it was the way they communicated.

I know they thought I was lucky to have been adopted but they didn't know anything about my life. They didn't see all the ins and outs of Dad being an alcoholic and Mum leaving when I was six. They didn't see how I near enough brought myself up and fell pregnant at 14. I didn't explain. I was so wrapped up in meeting everyone and finding things out that I didn't make a point of pushing that information home.

I hoped that everything would be perfect and happy, but it was impossible to find any balance especially when so much had happened to us all. I was naïve to think that it would be happy families. I am only okay now because of the extensive therapy I have had later in life. Before therapy, I was a screamer, which enabled me to let my emotions out. Maybe my sisters were screamers too.

I never did get to meet my brother Anthony; and very sadly I was to find out that he hung himself when he was younger. My adoptive sister Jacky found out by obtaining his death certificate. I don't know how it had occurred to her that he'd died. She likes to get to the bottom of things. I've gathered various certificates over the years. I got Anthony's birth certificate. He had lived near Lewes. I don't even have a picture of him.

CHAPTER TWELVE

By the mid-90s I had been dreaming of meeting my mother for more than 20 years. Would I look like her? Would she look like me?

The first time I went looking, I hunted for her around the Brixton area. I must have got this information from one of my siblings. I can't remember exactly what year in the 90s this was; but I went to all the shops and asked around. I didn't ask in the launderette as I just assumed she'd have a washing machine and a tumble dryer! Later I was to find out that if I had have done that, I would have found her earlier. Eventually we did get to find someone helpful who directed us to a block of flats nearby, so I just knocked on all these doors asking about her.

Karen came with me and eventually an older Rastafarian man opened the door, and he knew Maureen! We ended up going to the pub around the corner with him for a drink and he told us that Maureen had lived with him, but it was all over between them and that they hadn't had a good relationship. He couldn't tell us a lot, but he did say she might be living in a block of flats called Holt House.

I went to Holt House on the second occasion that I went looking, and this time I was with Jill and Jacky. We knocked on countless doors. "Excuse me but do you know Maureen..." I remember then reeling off all of the surnames that she may have been known as. Eventually, a man answered the door and it's so difficult to put into words, the emotions, when he not only said that yes, he did know her, but also that she was inside his flat.

*

"If you'd gone in the launderette, you would have found me sooner," she said.

There she was. Maureen McKilbride. I was 28 and finally meeting the woman who gave birth to me. I had always pictured her as glamorous. I just thought she'd be beautiful. But I couldn't have been more wrong. She was the total opposite - overweight, teeth missing, bad hair. It was just horrendous. And worse, I could really see me in her, which was scary because I'd never want to look like that. I knew she was vulnerable, of course, it was obvious, and I felt so sorry for her. I would have given her everything. I thought, *my god. I'm going to have to look after her for the rest of my life.* She was calm and asked me in for a chat. I think she was in shock. She didn't talk to me about her feelings or apologise in anyway. She did speak about her sister who was a London bus driver, and that they had fallen out. She spoke to me about Ricky. It was the main conversation. We went to the high street together, and I bought her some cigarettes. After that visit, she wouldn't stop ringing me. It was really difficult. I did tell my mum and dad, but they were very relaxed about it all.

Not long after I met Maureen, Susan gave me the heartbreaking news that Ricky had died. He and I had never seen each other after we met, that one time. We'd had that one hour together and I never saw him again. I went to see his girlfriend who lived in Crouch End. She had photos of Ricky which she offered to give me. "Take them," she said. But I only took one. I regret not taking more. I then told Maureen about Ricky and she was devastated, just screaming down the phone. I went to see her after this and could see how utterly distraught she was.

None of my sisters were in touch with Maureen. They all really hated her. I felt strangely sorry for Maureen, even after everything she had done. I know that if you have six children and you put them all into care, you're not going to be mentally stable. During this same period of time, Debbie came down a couple of times and stayed with me. Maureen was in Maudsley Mental Health hospital, by this time and we went to visit her. I was excited to see Maureen, but she was really horrible to Debbie. Debbie was petrified of her –really scared. Maureen started shouting at her. Debbie was understandably angry about having been put in foster care, which had so many dire consequences for her, Jackie and Susan, and confronted Maureen about it, which started a big argument. Debbie left saying, "She's going to hunt me down!"

Jackie wanted to come down to London to meet Maureen too. She hadn't seen her since she was very young. So, I contacted Maureen and told her, "Jackie wants to come down and see you." She told me then that Jackie wasn't really her baby. It was really weird, and I felt I couldn't let Jackie walk into that situation, so I told her, "She's saying really weird things. She's saying she's not your mum, that she wasn't really pregnant, and she pretended she was pregnant to keep her boyfriend."

Maureen told me that Jackie was her friend's baby and her friend had given her to her to care for. I knew this was a lie because Maureen was pregnant with another child when I was a baby as confirmed in my records. Why she made this story up I don't know. Maureen just didn't seem to want anything to do with Jackie. All due to her fragile mental state,

I suppose. But the outcome was awful, and it caused so much pain for Jackie and trouble between her and me. Part of me thinks I didn't think it through, I was young, and information was flying at me. I was trying to protect Jackie, but it probably didn't seem that way to her. Susan rang me and asked why I had told Jackie what Maureen had said. But supposing I'd said nothing, and Jackie had gone there. What about if Maureen had shut the door in her face and said that she'd told me that she didn't want to see Jackie? Wouldn't that have been more cruel and much worse? I feel I was punished for Maureen's decision, and I never spoke to any of my birth sisters again after that.

I was very sad because before this Debbie and her son had been to stay with me, and he and Michael had started to get to know each other as the cousins they are. I had started babysitting for Susan's children and we had become very close. It's a huge shame that Susan couldn't see her way past that argument between me and Jackie. I often think that I could probably get into contact with her, but I fear it would be opening another can of worms. I keep looking her up to see if she's still at her old address, but it seems she has moved and gone off the radar. I don't think she lives far away because she's definitely a London girl. I feel sure she's around here somewhere. As well as her two sons, but she could have had other children too. She was very maternal, and her house was so lovely. She decorated it herself and was a very talented, natural artist.

I met Maureen three times in total – the first time at her flat, then in the Maudsley and once after that when she had moved into a new flat after another relationship breakdown.

She then started phoning me all the time again. It was too much. One day I was driving along the Edgware Road, Cricklewood and I saw her number come up on my mobile. I told myself, *I can't even answer it. I can't talk to her.* So I didn't. That is the last time I heard from her. I've kept the same number but nobody – not Maureen, Debbie, Jackie or Susan – has contacted me since this time.

CHAPTER THIRTEEN

Amidst all this, in 1995, when I was 29, I met Anthony at the Middlesex and Herts country club. By this time, Karen had had twin daughters and the father was a good friend of Anthony's. Karen's daughters are called Jodie and Ellie. I have a particularly special relationship with Ellie. I love Jodie to bits but me and Ellie have just got this bond. It's another link between Karen and I that we had children with men who were friends. Not that I dreamt I would go out with, or marry Anthony, when I met him. Never. Around three months after meeting them at the club every week, we went to a pub together. We got chatting and I found him really funny. We have been together ever since. From day one he was great with Michael, who was 14 at the time. They've never fallen out. Michael and Mick's relationship stayed the same, very close. Mick had two boys with Debbie, giving Michael younger brothers.

Anthony is a scaffolder by trade. He grew up in

Willesden and Kilburn with his mum and his siblings. A short while after we met, he moved into my north Finchley flat with me. He would walk to the station, Woodside Park, every day to go to work and I would pick him up every evening from the station. We had a small, quiet wedding in June 2003 and Jodie and Ellie were my bridesmaids.

In those early days, Anthony and I spent our time together in the pub playing pool. We also went to pubs around Ladbrook Grove and hung out with his dad. At that time, Anthony worked for West 3 Scaffolding but then started working for himself. He's always worked really hard and still does, which affords us a lovely life together. We left the flat in Finchley, and bought a house together in Barnet just before we got married.

Coincidently, Anthony, did know of Susan, as believe it or not he had met her once, through his brother! I didn't know they knew each other until later.

Anthony and I were together a long time before I fell pregnant. To be honest, I thought I was happy with just Michael and Anthony wasn't fussed about having kids. But then we went to Spain, and I felt really sick. I had an inkling I was pregnant and when we came back, I had a test at the doctors. I was pregnant and we were both delighted. But then I had a miscarriage. We didn't tell anyone about it. I just spent the night in Barnet Hospital and even though I was treated terribly by the staff there, I coped okay. I just think these things happen in life.

After the miscarriage, we tried again but it didn't happen. I was going to go through IVF, so I had blood tests done. I saw one of the top IVF specialists in London who was amazing. But then at the last minute – I'd bought all the drugs and everything, which cost a fortune – I had a smear test. The test came back as positive for pre-cancerous cells for which treatment was needed. I'd had that before, about three times, but it meant the IVF had to be put on hold. I had the treatment for the cells and then I fell pregnant with Faye without IVF. I couldn't believe it. She was born on July 5, 2006.

I had a really easy pregnancy with Faye even though I was 39. We registered Faye on my 40th birthday, then Anthony took me to Jamie Oliver's restaurant 15 and then to Tiffany's to buy a necklace – silver with stars on. It was a perfect day.

After we had Faye, I fell pregnant again. I went to the Portland Hospital to have the scans and they discovered too much fluid at the back of the baby's neck and the consultant advised me to have a termination. That was horrendous because we really wanted the baby and had heard the heartbeat. But the doctors said the baby would have had something called Turner's Syndrome, which I later discovered is not that bad. That was really hard to deal with. I never got over that. I kept thinking, *I should never have had the termination.* Faye was two at the time, and in the room waiting for me when I woke up from the anesthetic. We tried again but I didn't fall pregnant, so it wasn't meant to be. Faye, as soon as she could talk, wanted a baby brother or sister. I felt bad not giving her one but then I think, *If I did have another one, she wouldn't be in this situation she's in now having had the opportunity to go to an independent school and concentrate on her drama and performing arts.* She is very much involved in this now, as well as her horses, and extremely happy.

Faye was incredibly shy when she was little, which is amazing compared to how confident she is now. She is very much like Anthony temperament wise, and unphased by things that some kids would be. I'm very glad about this as I want her to be happy and not suffer anxiety or emotional turmoil.

From the moment I found out I was pregnant I really wanted a girl. I just thought, *please let it be a girl.* I think with girls you have a different kind of relationship than with a son and I wanted that. It has been such an amazing experience having her. It's been so lovely. She has never caused me any trouble. Touch wood! Even when she was a baby, a toddler, she never had tantrums or anything. She cried if she fell over for instance, but she'd never have a tantrum and scream and say, "I want that!"

When Faye was born, we still lived in Barnet, but afterwards we moved to Goffs Oak in Hertfordshire. On my birthday a few years previously, Michael had surprised me with a beautiful black Labrador puppy. We called her Mollie and we all loved her very much. She only lived until she was 10, but she did move to Goffs Oak with us, which was wonderful for her as she had a few years really enjoying the huge field behind our house.

Faye's relationship with my dad is really wonderful to see. It's amazing. He loves her so much and she loves him. He's been there for her since she was born.

Faye was 16 in 2022 and I love to spoil her. She had a lovely party at home with a few friends and I bought her a puppy, Polo, to keep Oslo, our other dog, company. I love ensuring that she has everything she needs.

I love that I have been able to give Faye the life I would have wanted for myself. I pay attention to her life and know the things she likes and the things she doesn't. Nobody did that for me. I give her every opportunity that I can. I get such joy from seeing her happy and do everything in my power to give her a good life. I do things I wish my mum had done for me, even just simple things like picking her up from school. That's why I don't do a full-time job. I couldn't relax if I couldn't be there for her, making sure she's safe and knowing that she is wanted and most importantly, cherished. I love being around her. I miss her when I'm not with her. I'm her little mini cab driver – but I don't think she takes it for granted. I want her to have that security.

CHAPTER FOURTEEN

As happy as I was in my life with Anthony and Faye, and the pride I felt at watching Michael progress in his career in the Metropolitan Police, about six years ago, a sense of unease crept up on me. I felt immense shame at having been such a young mum. It didn't bother me as a young girl, and it hadn't bothered me for years, but it began when Faye started at her independent school. It was a really small school where everybody knew each other. As parents get to know each other, they ask perfectly normal questions like, "Have you got any other children?" And when you say that you do, they then ask "Oh, how old are they?"

Oh my God! I used to try and avoid people at all costs because I just didn't want to answer that question. People judge. Everyone does and I was completely paranoid about telling people I had a much older son, which would then reveal how young I would have to have been when I had him. One day Michael came to the school to watch

Faye's Christmas concert and one of the mums I was friendly with, recognised him. She also worked for the MET. She said, "Michael, what are you doing up here?" And he looked at me and I was like, "He's my son." She looked at me in total shock. She couldn't believe it.

Nothing changed and I'm still friends with her now. She never asked me how old I was when I had Michael so I suppose she might have assumed I was 17 or something. But that incident did nothing to allay my fears.

I was always on a knife edge, feeling anxious all day and having regular panic attacks. I tried to keep busy by going for walks. I felt that if I stopped, I was going to have a panic attack and that my life would be ruined yet again. It took time to recover from them and it was hard to live with the fear of it happening. I couldn't even help myself by watching anything to do with panic attacks or even reading about them as I was convinced that would trigger an attack. They could happen whenever. It was not that something had stressed out me in particular, it seemed to be underlying and the panic would grip me almost out of nowhere, without reason. I would feel my whole body go cold and I knew what was coming next.

There's always a straw the breaks the camel's back, isn't there? I was staying at my dad's in Burnt

Oak and taking Faye to her school – Sylvia Young Theatre School. The drive was a nightmare and as soon as I hit the Hendon Way going up to the Finchley Road, the traffic was solid. Someone pulled out of a turning and a bike tried to miss them and hit my car on the side. It wasn't my fault, but I was involved, I had to stop, and the police came. Part of it was probably that I had promised myself that I would always protect Faye from the dangers of life. That day, I hadn't been able to live up to my promise. It wasn't my fault, these things happen, but that was irrelevant to me because Faye was really scared, and I hated that. The motorcyclist was in the road, injured, the police were sat in my car talking to me.

It was traumatic and it terrified me. And I decided then and there that I couldn't be driving that journey every day. Fortunately, we were in a position to buy a flat in St John's Wood, which meant Faye and I could stay there during the week and avoid all the driving. When Covid hit and Faye had to study online, we rented it out.

Someone had hit my car before that as well. I was stationary, another driver was going too fast, someone pulled out and the fast driver swerved to avoid him and hit me. I started to feel like my anxiety levels were out of my control and inside, deep down, I knew that I needed help.

One day I saw a woman called Mandy Saligari on the television and I knew she was going to be the one to help me. The programme was called Celebs in Therapy and there on my screen were Daniella Westbrook, Paul Burrell, Danielle Lloyd and Gemma Collins. Apart from Daniella Westbrook – who was in a bad way obviously because of the drugs – I couldn't believe the others were there and I thought, *Jesus Christ. You're in therapy?*

Mandy, I learned, is an addiction, parenting and relationships expert. I thought: *If she's on TV helping them then surely, she can help me?* I decided to give her a ring at Charter Harley Street where she is the clinical director. But it took me so long to pick up the phone and even when I managed that, I couldn't dial the number. But eventually, after calling on January 20, 2017, I managed to make an appointment. Anthony drove me there and waited outside while I went in. Before I found Mandy and her team, I had seen my doctor and told him, "Literally, I can't cope. Please can you let me go into a hospital or somewhere where they can look after me."

Wanting to be placed in a mental health facility was a desperate grab at just not wanting to feel the way I was feeling – and being in that state. I needed it to stop, and I would have tried anything to just not feel how I felt. I was deeply unhappy and living in constant fear.

"You would not want to go into one, you really wouldn't," my doctor said.

"Really?"

"No." That put me off. It scared me to be honest.

I shook through the whole appointment with Mandy, crying as I told her bits about my life and she said, "You need to see Tanya." So I saw a therapist called Tanya and I joined the Women's Group with Tanya and another Therapist called Nalini. I began seeing Nalini one-to-one and a Therapist called Tom. Then Nalini left and I was referred to Kevin, which was amazing. I saw him one-to-one and he made a huge difference to me – they all did, to be fair. To this day if I had the money, I would see Kevin every week, but I just can't afford to. He is just amazing.

I was terrified at the prospect of going for therapy. Really anxious. And I would encourage people to listen to your gut, who you do and don't click with, but also to challenge yourself as much as you can and to listen to the advice that you're given. I felt that I didn't click with Tanya, but her advice to join the group was spot on. "Once you start talking about things and hearing other people talk you realise that everyone has got a few problems in their lives," she told me. "It will be good for you that you go into a group."

The group ran for 10 weeks and was the weirdest experience I'd ever had. I could barely open my mouth, yet I was supposed to be there, sharing the shameful details of my life and my feelings with eight complete strangers. I sat there saying barely a word and every week it got worse. The others would go round in a circle and talk about their lives, what was going on, but I found it impossible to join in. Sometimes I would walk out in the middle of the group sessions. Then I'd have them ringing and ringing me, but I couldn't answer. Eventually they would email and say, "You really need to come back to the group. Please come back." They were so lovely and kind. I'd go back. Sometimes I'd be crying the whole time, I was in such a state. My main issue, as always, was having Michael at a young age. But I couldn't even say it out loud. If I hadn't have had Faye and been made to face these simple but terrifying questions about the ages of any other children I had, I would have probably just plodded on and been a wreck of a person having panic attacks. I would have dealt with it in my own way. Or rather, I wouldn't have dealt with it.

There were people in there who took drugs, there was alcohol related trauma and basically people from all walks of life. People had been through horrific experiences. I wasn't alone. But still I wasn't ready to open up.

I must have fallen out with my adoptive mum Janice a bit before this because I phoned her when I got back from going to see Mandy, when I understood what this therapy was going to cost. Mandy had asked me, "Can you afford this?" And I said, "Well I will *have* to find the money." I phoned my mum when I got home because she had just sold her house. "Can you pay some money toward my therapy?" I asked her. "I think you should."

She never *ever* calls me Denise. She usually calls me Neecy. But on this occasion, she did. She was furious and she's not an angry person. I've never heard her lose her temper very much. She's very calm and she doesn't really raise her voice.

"I will transfer your money over, Denise," she said. I knew she was extremely angry. I thought, *My God, we've fallen out over money.*

I calmed down and a few days later I texted her and said: "I don't want your money." I didn't take it from her. That was it. I think I saw her once after that and everything was okay until I opened that letter. Until then I had vowed never to fall out with her again; I just thought, *What's the point?* But whenever I talk to her it's always, "Jill and Jacky... Jill took me here." It's sort of a bit of a jealousy thing as well, so I think, *What's the point? I can't actually deal with it.*

I'm happier now, not being involved in all of their lives. I don't have to worry about what they're doing and what they're not doing. It works well for me.

CHAPTER FIFTEEN

EMDR (Eye Movement Desensitization and Reprocessing) is a psychotherapy that enables people to heal from the symptoms and emotional distress that are the result of disturbing life experiences.

Repeated studies show that by using EMDR therapy, people can experience the benefits of psychotherapy that once took years to make a difference. It is widely assumed that severe emotional pain requires a long time to heal. EMDR therapy shows that the mind can in fact heal from psychological trauma much as the body recovers from physical trauma.

When you cut your hand, your body works to close the wound. If a foreign object or repeated injury irritates the wound, it festers and causes pain. Once the block is removed, healing resumes.

EMDR therapy demonstrates that a similar sequence of events occurs with mental processes. The brain's information processing system naturally moves toward mental health. If the system is blocked or imbalanced by the impact of a disturbing event, the emotional wound festers and can cause intense suffering. Once the block is removed, healing resumes. Using the detailed protocols and procedures learned in EMDR therapy training sessions, clinicians help clients activate their natural healing processes.

More than 30 positive controlled outcome studies have been done on EMDR therapy. Some of the studies show that 84%-90% of single-trauma victims no longer have post-traumatic stress disorder after only three 90-minute sessions.

From: https://www.emdr.com/what-is-emdr/

I first had EMDR treatment on May 25, 2017 while I was still in the women's group. I'd never even heard of it before. I had to imagine me at a certain stage in my life, so I remembered this photo I have of myself where I look so sad, like a little orphan. I pictured that in my brain and then imagined my Mum, Janice there too. And I bent down, as adult me now, and picked baby me up and cuddled her, to try and make baby Denise feel loved, safe and comforted.

It was deeply traumatic. I was just a complete mess. I cried the whole session with the pain of feeling what I must have felt as a baby and how that affected every part of me. The pain, the sense of loss, separation, abandonment and the lack of love, which babies crave and need to physically develop. It was awful. But I came out the other side eventually.

It's probably hard for people to understand the therapy I had and to be honest, I didn't really get it myself. I'm one of these people who walks into things and realises what it's all about later. Maybe I'm not focused enough. Or maybe it's because it's complicated. But it takes a while for things to get through to my brain. It seems that although I had sought therapy for the shame I felt as a young mum, it was my feelings of being unworthy from a young age due to the complicated situation with my birth and adoptive parents, that was actually causing the sense of being unloved and therefore shame that threatened to overwhelm me.

But it absolutely 100 per cent worked. I had to nurture myself and make me feel better. Tom the therapist was absolutely amazing and not every session was focused on my mother. We talked about other things. I had six sessions with him, and they were all EMDR. It was £230 a session and worth every single penny. I just wished that I'd met all of those people earlier.

Tom told me, "There's nothing to be ashamed of having a baby at that age. You brought him up well. He's a police officer." He just made me feel so much better about myself. It only takes one person, really, to turn your life around, to give you that support. I'd never had that. I've never had anybody say, "That is amazing. You've brought up a human being who is protecting the public." I thought, *Yeah, actually.*

After I had EMDR I attended my school reunion. It was amazing. I loved it! I told people, "Well, I was pregnant at school." A lot of them didn't realise.

Today, I'll tell people, "Yeah. I had Michael when I was 15." Then I say he's been in the Met for 20 years. I remember when he told me he wanted to join the police. I was amazed. His passing out parade at Hendon was a day I'll never forget. I'm proud of him and he's done well. It's a nice feeling, whereas I've always hidden it.

I had come to wish I'd had Michael at 17 because that's acceptable. I think 15 is so young and I was pregnant at 14. It is *too* young. Even though I felt when I was 14 that I was 18. I always felt older. I didn't feel like a little schoolgirl. But then, look at the childhood I'd had, or rather not had.

I attended lots of other workshops too. One I was referred to was anger management and I refused. I reacted really badly, which probably showed that I needed to go! I rejected that I needed it because when you're told, "You've got to go on an anger management course," it's quite scary. And it put my back up. "How *dare* you say I need that? I'm not angry!" Of course, I was angry. Are you mad? I was the angriest person in the world.

I understand anger now, I know that you have to have it. It's a feeling and we shouldn't be ashamed of it. We just have to use it appropriately. My therapist said to me that my anger kept me alive. I didn't know that. Instead of going out gambling and taking drugs or drinking alcohol, anger kept me alive. 100 per cent.

If I could go back and do the anger management, I would.

Not that I got into fights or anything like that, but I definitely had a short fuse growing up, and obviously with Mick, he knew how to press those buttons by his taunts. You're not going to laugh it off, are you.

As part of my therapy, I went on a weekend long Parenting From Within course at Harley Street. It was intense. If I'd have known what it was going to be like I probably wouldn't have done it. It cost a lot of money as well. There were three other ladies there. Basically, you choose one person to focus on. I chose my mum, Janice. To this day, I really don't know why. I should have chosen my dad, but I thought, *I'll choose my mum because I don't see her that often and I can cope with the relationship with my dad.* But really, I should have had it with my dad, and we would have had a much better relationship.

If I'd never gone for therapy, then God knows what I'd be like. Completely messed-up still, I expect. I wouldn't say I'm 100 per cent because I have my wobbly days, but obviously I am getting there. My therapy lasted two years from 2017 to 2019.

CHAPTER SIXTEEN

Thank God for therapists. I know I can always phone them. That is a lifeline to me. And today if someone knows me as Faye's mum and asks if I have any other children, I don't hide away from it and change the subject. I will say it, but I don't give the information if someone isn't asking for it. I'm less worried about it and it helps that Faye tells me, "Mum, don't worry about what anyone thinks." She's very much like that. If somebody asked me now, I would say, "Yeah, I was a teenage mum." It wouldn't bother me.

I've been on Tik Tok a fair bit recently, more so during the lockdown. And you get these girls who are 15 and have children. The support that they get is overwhelming. It's unbelievable. I'm like, *Oh my God. I really didn't think people would think like that.* It's crazy. People say: *Well done! Take care! You're amazing!* Really none of the comments are horrible. It's eye opening. I write supportive comments too. I would never want anyone to feel how I felt for all those years. To give them support feels amazing. I read the comments and think, *Oh my God. There are so many kind people out there wishing the best for this girl.*

I lived my life like a different person before therapy. I could never, ever be relaxed and myself. That's only come out since I finished therapy; that I could actually relax and think, *I am who I am, and I don't care who is going to judge me.* It really doesn't bother me now.

Faye is surrounded by family, her dad and I, her lovely big brother, her two nephews and of course she's very close to my dad, which is lovely. He's 93 now and he's not going to live forever so I'm dreading what she'll be like when we lose him. But she's sensible so hopefully she'll get through it okay. Thankfully, my issues definitely didn't affect Michael.

I still get anxious and stressed about small things but nowadays, I calm down pretty quickly and can rationalise.

Faye can sometimes say to me, "I'm so stressed," and I hear her friends saying on the phone to her. "I'm so bloody anxious."

I tell her, "Faye, don't use that word 'anxious', you're just a little tiny bit stressed because of homework or whatever." I don't want her saying all this. I don't want her to use that word flippantly. It *is* a real thing. Say you're a bit stressed with homework, that's fine. But you're not anxious, Faye. No, you're not. Anxiety is totally different.

I can only now speak about panic attacks. I feel as if there's this little person on my shoulder who says, "Don't push your luck because if you do, you're going to have one." But I can respond to that voice and say, *It's fine. You're fine. Don't worry. You're in control.*

CHAPTER SEVENTEEN

I have never talked to dad about my therapy. When I felt really ill years ago, he actually wrote me a letter which I've never opened. That was about 20 years ago.

I think at the time it was because, if he'd written about mental health issues, that would have panicked me when I needed him to be strong for me. I've never known him to go into hospital or have any help with that. He was definitely an alcoholic though.

But to everyone's amazement, Dad stopped drinking when I was 31. I'd been with Anthony for a couple of years by then and Dad just woke up one morning, said, "I'm not drinking again." And he didn't. Just like that. I just think he'd had enough. It wasn't doing him any favours. He never went in the pub again. A lot of his mates down the pub had died and I think he worried about what the booze was doing to him. All of his money had gone down the drain too.

I was so happy for him. When my dad was a drunk, he didn't really talk that much, and you couldn't really get a sentence out of him. But now he's stopped drinking, he hasn't stopped talking, but that's been lovely and has massively improved our relationship. I am so happy that he's still alive at 93!

I love him because he tried his best for me. Growing up, I idolised him. If I ever argued with my mum I'd tell her, "Dad does everything for me." It wasn't until I got older that I really understood this wasn't the norm! Now that he's sober, he will do anything for me. I've seen a new side to him. If I phone him and say, "Dad, can you see if you can get me this book," he'll hunt it down for me and get it. That would be his mission for the day. Funny isn't it.

In 2019, Dad told me that his brother, whose name is Norman but nicknamed Whip, was in hospital in Great Yarmouth and really down in the dumps having given up on life. He's a year younger than my dad. "He's given up on everything. I don't think he's going to come out of hospital," Whip's daughter Lynne told my dad.

"Oh my God Dad, that's terrible," I said. "Do you want to go up there and see him?" Dad wasn't sure but I encouraged him and found out where Whip was, which ward. Dad and I drove up there.

It took two-and-a-half hours. We stayed there for about an hour. Then we drove home again so it was five hours in the car. My dad did not stop talking from the moment he got in that car until the moment we got back. Do you know what? He did not irritate me *once*. Not once. He didn't say anything I didn't agree with. He was talking all about his life, whom he'd met, what jobs he'd done. All about everything. As much as he has driven me mad and I do resent things, that journey really made a difference.

And Whip was really pleased to see him. The next Sunday I said, "Have you heard from Whip?" He said, "Yeah. I spoke to him yesterday. He's home and he actually went down the pub for a pint." There's Lynne phoning, saying he's on his deathbed! I said, "I told you, Dad!" When I saw him, I spoke to the nurse, and he said he's got a few things wrong with him but it's not life-threatening.

Me and my dad have had our ups and downs. I just want everything to run smoothly, bless him. He's got all his marbles. He's walking fine. He's healthy. He comes up to me every Saturday or Sunday and I give him breakfast or lunch. I might be okay, or I might feel resentful. I don't know my feelings until he knocks on the door. Sometimes I'm happy to see him, sometimes I can't even open the door. I have to let Faye open it or Anthony and then sometimes I can't go in the front room and talk to him, so Anthony does it for me. Other times I can go in the front room and talk to him. It just depends on what mood I'm in.

It's very rare for him to say, "I love you". Faye phones him up and says, "I love you, Grandad," and he'll say, "I love you too." But it's very hard for him to say that.

Michael has two sons now, Mikey who was born in 2011 and Louis who was born two years later. Becoming a nanny was a bit of a challenge and when I'm out and about with them I sometimes joke about and ask them to call me Neecy instead of Nanny!

Unfortunately, Michael had now fallen out with his dad. Quite recently, Mick bought Michael's girlfriend Iwona a bangle for her 40th birthday. Iwona told Michael that while it was a lovely present, she didn't think she would wear it. She wondered if Mick might exchange it for a necklace or earrings that she would wear. Michael approached Mick and he was happy to do this. But about a month later, Michael was at his dad's and saw the bangle and receipt in the kitchen. Mick wasn't home so Michael rang him and asked if he'd tried to exchange it and Mick said the shop wouldn't allow it. Michael told Mick, "Oh, I'll take it then." And no more was said. Then, about 10 months later, Mick rang Michael and asked him where the bangle was. Michael reminded his dad that he'd taken the bangle as agreed by him, but Mick wasn't having any of it and was totally vile and abusive to Michael, calling him a thief. He also sent disgusting messages to Iwona who couldn't believe what was implying. I was beyond furious that Mick could call Michael, a Met police officer, a thief, and was reminded of exactly what sort of person Mick is.

Since writing this, my dad has moved into assisted living, just around the corner from me. It's lovely there and his flat is perfect. I go there most days and do everything for him: shopping, appointments, dog walking – cleaning and washing. Dad is happy there with us all around the corner.

One thing I find extremely difficult is how little my sisters Jacky and Jill see our dad now. Its been 6 years since they have seen him. This is such a shame.

Jacky, Jill and my mum, all now live in Wales and have got a very close relationship.

CHAPTER EIGHTEEN

I think about all my birth siblings all the time and just recently, I contacted Debbie. We had a lovely conversation and hope to meet up soon.

I don't feel thankful that I was adopted. I really don't. As much as I might have had a worse life being in care, it's hard for me to feel grateful as too much has happened.

If my birth mother Maureen called me now, I really don't how I would react. She doesn't cross my mind nowadays. I did try ringing her a few years ago – but the landline just rang and rang. Maybe she doesn't even live in that flat anymore. Or maybe she has died. I feel fine about it either way.

When I see lovely families with mums and dads and brothers and sisters and they're all happy. I think, *I would have loved that. Imagine having that growing up.* Having that security. People don't realise. I think they take it for granted. They don't realise how lucky they are to have a mum and a dad who are still together. Brothers and sisters that they get on with.

I am proud that I have been able to create the childhood for Michael and Faye that I would have wanted for myself. I've had crazy times, but I've been responsible and nurturing towards my children. And I have nurtured myself with therapy and I hope I can continue with it again one day as I feel so much lighter as a result of that help.

I love my children more than I can express. Michael and Faye have a wonderful relationship. A few years ago, the three of us went to Corfu together and honestly, it was magical. I was never mothered but motherhood wasn't a struggle for me, and I will always be grateful for that. And maybe even a little bit proud of myself too.

ACKNOWLEDGMENTS

Thank you to my best friend, Karen, who helped me remember so much, and to my husband, Anthony, for all his love and support.

ABOUT THE AUTHOR

Denise Larkin was born in 1966 in Kingsbury, London, and a few months later moved the Watling Estate in Burnt Oak to live with her adoptive parents Ray and Janice Best, and their daughters Jacky and Jill. She has two children, Michael and Faye, and lives with her husband Anthony in Goffs Oak, Hertfordshire with their dogs. This is her first book.

Printed in Great Britain
by Amazon